GEORGE ANCONA

CUTTERS, CARVERS & THE CATHEDRAL

LOTHROP, LEE & SHEPARD BOOKS

My thanks go to the people who made this book possible.
To Ann Walters, who first introduced me to Indiana limestone. To Suzanne Bronski and Bill Logan,
of the Cathedral Church of Saint John the Divine, who smoothed my path to the stone yard. To the men
and women who work in the stone yard, for sharing their time and experience with me. To Pamela
Duffy and Claudio Edinger, my hosts in New York. To Laura Bybee and her husband, Will Bybee, who
were so gracious on my visit to the Bybee Stone Company; to Shannon Barnes, who guided me through
the Indiana Limestone Company; and to Josh, Bruce, and Sheila Poole.

Inquiries should be addressed to Lothrop, Lee & Shepard Books,
a division of William Morrow & Company, Inc.,
1350 Avenue of the Americas, New York, New York 10019.
Printed in the United States of America
First Edition   1 2 3 4 5 6 7 8 9 10
Library of Congress Cataloging in Publication Data
Ancona, George.
Cutters, carvers, & the cathedral / George Ancona.
p.   cm.
ISBN 0-688-12056-3. — ISBN 0-688-12057-1 (lib. bdg.)
1. Cathedrals-New York (N.Y.)—Design and construction—Juvenile
literature. 2 Stone cutters—New York (N.Y.)—Juvenile literature.
3. Stone carvers—New York (N.Y.)—Juvenile literature.
4. Cathedral of St. John the Divine (New York, N.Y.)—Juvenile
literature. [1.Cathedrals. 2. Stone cutters. 3. Stone carvers.
4. Cathedral of St. John the Divine (New York, N.Y.)] I. Title.
TH4221.A53 1995 693'.1—dc20 94-10549   CIP   AC

To Tana Hoban

Perched on the scaffolding in front of the giant bronze doors of the Cathedral of Saint John the Divine, Simon Verity works at carving the limestone columns with a chisel and mallet. So intent is this master carver on his work that he barely hears the noise of the New York City traffic below. For more than one hundred years, since long before Simon was born, the cathedral has been rising, stone upon stone,...and it is still not finished.

It takes many people to build a cathedral: architects, engineers, carpenters, glass makers, electricians, masons, quarriers. And it takes a tremendous amount of stone. Most of the limestone for Saint John comes from far-away Indiana.

Bruce Poole works as a machinist in an Indiana quarry mill. During the summer, his son Josh likes to join him for lunch. They sit together on a limestone block to eat and watch the crew at work. Many of the workers trace their family roots to quarriers who sailed from England to America in the early nineteenth century. Sons work alongside their fathers and grandfathers, cutting giant blocks of limestone from the earth. Someday Josh may work in the quarry too.

A warning whistle sounds and everyone leaves the area. After a moment of silence, the earth rumbles. Dynamite charges explode on the far side of the quarry, uncovering a new section of the limestone seam.

When the rain of stone and dirt stops, a giant power shovel moves in to scoop up the overburden of earth and load it into the hauler trucks that take it away. It may take weeks to expose the high-quality limestone. Someday, this stone will be part of a skyscraper, a museum,...or the Cathedral of Saint John the Divine.

Once the seam is cleared, the saw runners take over. These are the men who operate the fifteen-foot diamond-tipped saw, cutting blocks called ledges into the stone. Each block is as long as two school buses.

The quarry bursts with the roar of pneumatic drills as drill runners drive holes into the base of the ledge where it is still attached to the seam.

The drill runners are followed by the breakers, who set steel wedges into the holes. Then, swinging their sledge hammers, they pound the wedges into the stone, separating the ledge from the seam.

Mike Edwards has worked in the quarry as a laborer, drill runner, and breaker. "Each has its own skill," says Mike. "The breaker has to have a good 'lick' to hit those wedges just right, so the stone breaks in a straight line. We take the stone from the ground with drills, wedges, hammers, and sweat. It's a painful job and by the end of the day your hands are pretty numb."

Once the ledge is free, the crewmen slip flat rubber bags into the cuts that the saw runners made. As the bags are inflated by high-pressure hoses, they gradually push the ledge out, tipping it farther and farther. Finally it topples over and crashes to the ground in a cloud of dust.

As the air clears, David Prince, the quarry foreman, scrambles onto the ledge to mark out smaller blocks for the crew to cut. Often, they find fossils in the limestone and chip them out to save. Three million years ago, oceans covered the land we know as Indiana. As the waters receded, the prehistoric creatures that swam there were left on the ocean floor and their skeletons became solid limestone. "It's all those bones," says Dave. "That's why the limestone is so rich in calcium."

A loader picks up the smaller blocks and puts them onto flatbed trucks. Each truck can carry two of the 11 1/2-ton blocks across Indiana, Ohio, Pennsylvania, and New Jersey to New York City, where they will become part of the cathedral.

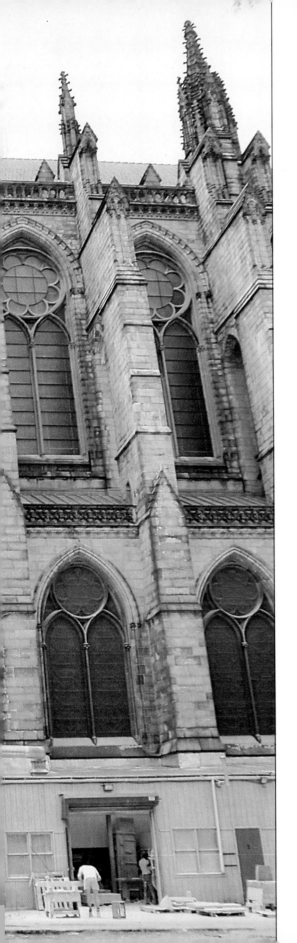

At the cathedral, where Edgar Reyes takes the blocks off the truck, scaffolds stand where towers will someday be. Still, even in its unfinished form, the cathedral soars above the surrounding neighborhood.

The cornerstone, the first stone of the building, was laid in 1892. It took fifty years—until November 30, 1941—to complete the main body of the church. The following Sunday, the Second World War broke out. No construction was done for thirty years, until the Very Reverend James Parks Morton became dean of the cathedral. Under the dean's leadership, a covered stone yard was built next to the cathedral and master stone carvers were invited from Europe to train neighborhood youths to become masons and carvers.

Edgar, one of the first neighborhood apprentices, also works in the machine shop, cutting up the huge blocks with the 11-foot circular saw. Computers control the saws that cut and shape the limestone into the precise forms called for by the architect's plans. These smaller blocks need very little hand finishing by the masons.

After years of learning his craft, Edgar's pride is obvious: "When I stand back and look at the cathedral, I can say, 'I did that!'"

Deep below the cathedral floor, "Jeep" Kincannon, the chief masonry draftsman, works in the architecture office. "To be a good mason, you must have a good sense of geometry," he says. "With the computer, I can produce the templates for the blocks that go into the cathedral.

The masons use these templates, or patterns, to shape each block of stone." All the blocks are cut to fit into their specific places, and they rise one above the other into columns, arches, walls, and steeples.

Through the haze of limestone dust, the early-morning sun sends shafts of light into the stone shed. Masons and carvers are busy working on blocks and sculptures. Their tools range from modern pneumatic drills and grinders to the traditional chisel and mallet.

Stephen Boyle, the stone–yard foreman, picks out a template for one of the masons. Stephen worked on the restorations of the twelfth-century Yorkminster and Salisbury cathedrals in England before coming to the United States. "Masons shape and finish the blocks," he explains, "while carvers cut intricate decorations for cornices, capitals, and pinnacles. On a pinnacle, the highest point on the cathedral, for example, it is the mason who cuts and assembles the blocks and the carver who cuts the crockets that go up the sides."

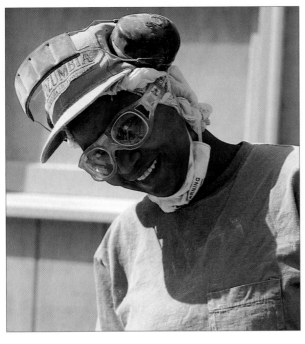

The men and women who work on the cathedral come from the neighborhood and from other countries as well, and they form their own small international community.

Wearing safety glasses, a hearing protector, and dust mask, Lisa Young finishes a block with sandpaper. When asked why she joined the apprenticeship program, she says, "I wanted a job that would give me the discipline to stay in school."

"When I first came to this country, I looked around for work," says Rafael Taverna, who grew up in Guatemala. "I saw the cathedral, came in, and there was an opening. I enjoy the work, to cut stone, to sculpt."

Michael Orekunrin left his native Nigeria after studying sculpture and carves blocks as an apprentice at Saint John.

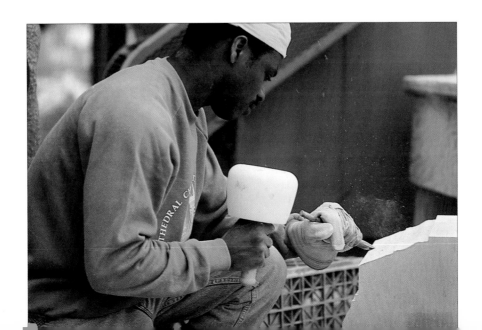

When he was sixteen, John Sutton worked in a quarry in England. He decided he liked working with stone and went to school to earn his mason's certificate. He uses an angle grinder to smooth out a stone he has cut.

"How did I fall in love with stone?" asks Amy Breyer, who has worked at the cathedral for five years. "I went to Italy and got my hands on a piece of marble and that was it."

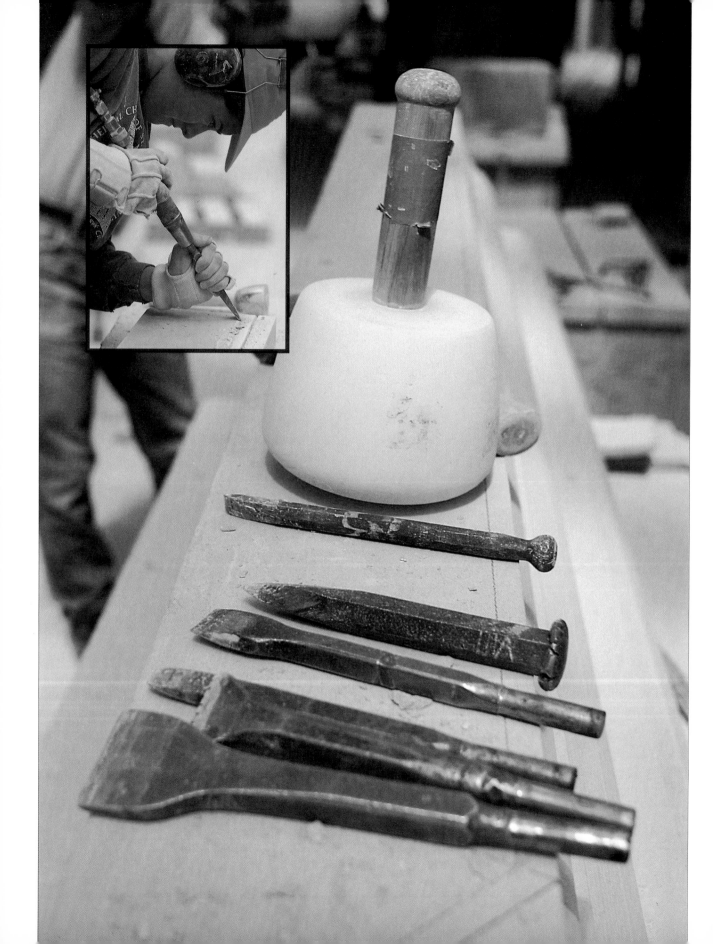

Jin Sheng Wong was a stone carver in China. For him, carving is a communication with the stone. "When I look at the stone, I can feel its power," he says while chiseling out a relief. "You cannot fight the stone. If you do, hitting it hard, your hand will get bloody. You've got to be gentle. To be a stone carver, you've got to love this kind of work. It's noisy, dusty, and hard."

Simon Verity comes down from the scaffolding to get a better view of his work and to talk of his career. "My family are French architects who have built cathedrals since the fourteenth century. As a boy I collected fossils, and I knew I'd be either a geologist or a sculptor. I'm mostly self-taught.

"To be a carver, you have to have a passion for it, to love it with all your heart. It's a desire to create order out of chaos, to seek harmonies. My figures are designed in relationship to the architecture and floor plan of the cathedral, and my tools are simply a hammer and chisel.

"My work as master carver is considered glamorous," he says. "But it is less important than the masons', who carve the blocks that hold the cathedral together."

Construction on the cathedral has stopped for lack of funding. Pinnacles, blocks, and gargoyles stand in the stone yard, awaiting the day when they will become part of the facade. Some of the figures portray leaders in the struggle for social justice, such as Nelson Mandela. Others represent some of the men and women who have worked on the cathedral.

Yet, services are held, concerts are performed, and festivals are celebrated. The helpless and homeless are fed, clothed, and befriended within its walls. Messages of peace and goodwill are sent out to the world.

It takes years of dedication and work, by people from near and far, to build the cathedral. But if the limestone took three million years to form, a hundred years to build a monument to faith doesn't seem so very long.

GLOSSARY

breaker a quarrier who sets and hammers steel wedges into stone in order to break it apart

capital the uppermost part of a column

cathedral a church that is the official seat of a bishop

chisel a metal carving tool with a cutting edge at the end of the blade

cornice a horizontal, often decorated piece at or near the top of a building or an architectural design

crocket an ornament, usually shaped like bent leaves, used on the edge of a gable or spire

draftsman (or draughtsman) one who draws the plans for a building

drill runner a quarrier who operates pneumatic drills

gargoyle a water spout in the form of a grotesque beast or human that projects from a roof

grinder a machine with a wheel that shapes and polishes stone

ledge a narrow, flat projection or layer of rock

mallet a hammer with a barrel-shaped head

mason a skilled worker who builds by laying one stone upon another

overburden material that lies over a useful layer of geological materials

pinnacle an upright architectural unit that often ends in a spire and is often at or near the top of a building

quarrier a worker in an excavation for obtaining stone

saw runner a worker who operates a saw that cuts into stone in a quarry

scaffold a temporary or moveable platform to stand or sit on when working above the ground

seam a thin layer of mineral matter in the earth

spire a tapering or pyramid-shaped roof on a tower; a steeple

template a pattern used as a guide to the cutting or shaping of stone or other material